HOW TO GET ALL THE CREDIT YOU WANT— And Erase Your Bad Credit Record

▼

HOW TO GET ALL THE CREDIT YOU WANT—
And Erase Your Bad Credit Record

▼
─────────────

Bob Hammond

A CITADEL PRESS BOOK
Published by Carol Publishing Group

Also by Bob Hammond:

How To Beat the Credit Bureaus:
The Insider's Guide to Consumer Credit

First Carol Publishing Group Edition 1993

A Citadel Press Book
Published by Carol Publishing Group
Citadel Press is a registered trademark of Carol Communications, Inc.
Editorial Offices: 600 Madison Avenue, New York, N.Y. 10022
Sales and Distribution Offices: 120 Enterprise Avenue, Secaucus, N.J. 07094
In Canada: Canadian Manda Group, P.O. Box 920, Station U, Toronto, Ontario M8Z 5P9
Queries regarding rights and permissions should be addressed to Carol Publishing Group,
600 Madison Avenue, New York, N.Y. 10022

First published as *Credit Secrets: How to Erase Bad Credit* by Paladin Press, Boulder,
Colorado, in 1989.

Neither the author nor the publisher assumes any responsibility for the use or misuse
of information contained in this book.

ISBN 0-8065-1397-7

Manufactured in the United States of America

10 9 8 7 6 5 4 3 2 1

CONTENTS

▼

WARNING

This book contains certain confidential information that could easily be subject to abuse or misuse. The author and publisher do not encourage, endorse, or recommend the use of any of these methods as a means to defraud or violate the rights of any individual or organization. The reader is therefore encouraged to use this material responsibly.

The author is not engaged in rendering any legal service. The services of a professional are recommended if legal advice or assistance is needed. The author and publisher disclaim any responsibility for personal loss or liabilities caused by the use or misuse of any information presented herein.

Inquiries and correspondence should be sent to the author in care of the publisher.

INTRODUCTION

▼

Have you ever been turned down for credit because of negative information contained in your credit report? I have. In fact, one of the most humiliating moments in my life occurred when I was told by a bank that I couldn't even open a savings account due to the negative information reported by a certain agency. I couldn't believe it!

I eventually was able to convince another bank to let me open an account. Several months later I requested a small loan in order to reestablish my credit. I even offered to let the bank freeze $1,000 that I had deposited as collateral. Again, I was turned down.

Can you imagine being turned down for trying to borrow your *own* money? The bank's reason? Negative information in credit bureau reports. In my case, the information was *very* negative: bankruptcy, charge-offs, collection accounts, and an overdrawn checking account. My credit was so bad, I was once told that I needed to come back with cash and two cosigners!

I won't go into the details of how I got myself into such

a financial mess right now (you'll have to wait until the movie comes out!). I only wish that I knew then what I know now and was aware of the information contained in this book. One thing I can say, however, is that if the methods outlined in this book could work miracles for me, they can work for *anybody*! And they will work for you, too.

I now have excellent credit. All of my old past-due accounts have been settled and marked "paid satisfactorily." I am free of all bad debts and money worries. I enjoy a comfortable living with income from several successful businesses, and I am well on my way to becoming a multimillionaire.

Over a period of years, I spent thousands of dollars attending seminars and consulting attorneys, financial consultants, and other self-proclaimed experts. I purchased every book and "underground" report I could find on the subjects of credit and consumer rights. Finally, after much investigative research, I discovered the closely guarded secrets used by the best credit consultants in the business; men and women who utilize the same dynamic techniques that are revealed in this book!

By carefully studying these techniques and by applying them to your own situation, you will be amazed at the results you can achieve in a short period of time. Once you become adept at some of the more advanced strategies, you may consider going into business for yourself as a professional credit consultant. Even as a casual sideline, this could mean several thousand dollars of extra income.

Some credit consultants earn over $100,000 a year. One woman in Los Angeles reports an income of over $20,000 a *week* using nothing more than the techniques revealed in this book. All it takes is specialized knowledge and a bit of faith in yourself. As Benjamin Franklin so aptly stated, "An investment in knowledge pays the best dividends."

Your decision to buy this book may well be one of the wisest choices you have ever made. In truth, you are investing in yourself and in your own unlimited potential. Begin now by setting a goal to improve your financial situation. For some of you it may mean simply paying off all your old debts. For others, it may include becoming financially independent in a business of your own.

Be as specific as possible. How much money do you want to earn this year? Now imagine yourself having accomplished your goal. What kind of car would you be driving? What kind of house would you live in? How much money would you have in the bank?

My hope is that today you will begin taking positive steps toward your increased prosperity. Yet this is not a program of positive thinking. Rather, it is a program of *positive action!* So act now! You are standing at the threshold of unlimited opportunity. The only limits are the ones you impose upon yourself. It is my privilege to offer what assistance I can on your road to success.

CHAPTER ONE
HOW DO YOU RATE?

▼

Recently, a young lady came to me in tears after being denied credit for a new car. She told me she was turned down because of a number of charge-offs and collection accounts on her credit report. She went on to explain that those accounts belonged to her ex-husband, who had agreed to pay them when they were divorced. Needless to say, his irresponsibility had caused serious damage to her credit rating. I reassured her that with a little time and effort, she would be able to finance any type of car she wanted. Three weeks later she took me out to dinner in her new BMW.

As you know, we live in a credit-oriented society. Most stores won't even accept a personal check without a major credit card to back it up. It is almost impossible to buy a house or car without obtaining some type of financing. Even renting an apartment takes good credit these days.

Negative credit information in your files—such as previous late payments, collection accounts, or judgments—can prevent a lender from even considering your credit application, regardless of your current ability to pay! In other cases, it can result in higher interest rates and extra fees (known as *points*). This can mean a difference of several thousand dollars on a large credit purchase, such as a new car or home.

If you're like 70 percent of all adult consumers, you have at least one item of negative information in your credit file. In many cases there is information that is incorrect, misleading, inaccurate, or obsolete. I have seen many credit reports on clients in which there is information about someone else with a similar name or Social Security number. In fact, so much incorrect information has been reported by one major credit bureau, it is rumored that their initials are an acronym for The Report is Wrong!

Credit bureaus (also known as *consumer reporting agencies*) make their money by compiling and selling information about you that has been reported to them by their subscribers. These subscribers include banks, department stores, finance companies, collection agencies, and mortgage companies. The information includes credit histories, account balances, and payment patterns.

The credit bureaus also receive and report public-record information. This includes bankruptcies, judgments, tax liens, wage garnishments, and notices of default. This information is generally gathered manually by low-paid clerks, which often leads to inaccurate information being reported in the consumer's credit file.

The information in your credit report is usually divided into three types of ratings: positive, neutral, and negative.

The following are the only statements on your credit report that are considered *positive*:

1. Paid satisfactorily or paid as agreed
2. Current account with no late payments
3. Account/credit line closed; consumer's request

The following statements are considered *neutral* (in

reality, anything less than a positive rating is considered negative by many credit grantors):

1. Paid; was 30 days late
2. Current; was 30 days late
3. Inquiry
4. Credit card lost
5. Refinance
6. Settled
7. Paid

The following statements are considered *negative*:

1. Bankruptcy; Chapter 7 or Chapter 13
2. Judgments
3. Tax liens
4. Account closed; grantor's request
5. Paid; was 60, 90, or 120 days late
6. SCNL; Subscriber Can Not Locate
7. Paid collection
8. Paid charge-off
9. Bk liq reo; bankruptcy liquidation
10. Charge-off
11. Collection account
12. Delinquent
13. Current; was 60, 90, or 120 days late
14. CHECKPOINT, TRANS ALERT, or CAUTION (potential fraud indicators)
15. Excessive inquiries (looks like you've been turned down by everyone else)

CHAPTER TWO
FREEDOM FROM DEBT

▼

For a long time I was deeply in debt without hope of breaking even. It felt like I was carrying a huge weight on my shoulders. I couldn't sleep at night. I was afraid to answer the phone. I was a nervous wreck! I even considered changing my name and leaving the state. The only thing that prevented me from disappearing and starting over was that I was totally broke. Unfortunately, so was my car.

One day I decided that no matter what it took, I would become free of all debts and money worries once and for all. I didn't know how I was going to do it. I just knew that somehow I would.

I developed a plan of action. I began by making a list of all of my financial obligations as well as my monthly income and expenses. Then I said a little prayer and asked God to help me see a way out of what appeared to be a hopeless situation.

I used various methods with different creditors to chip away at my debts. As time progressed, I updated my monthly income sheet and personal financial statement.

Each time, I noticed that my debts were growing smaller and my net worth was increasing. Before I realized it, I had completely eliminated all of my old past-due accounts. It was a miracle. I was free!

In the course of this experience, I learned several powerful techniques for negotiating with creditors. I also investigated a number of dynamic legal maneuvers for eliminating debt. The following is a summary of the methods I have found to be most effective.

The best way to deal with excessive debt is to avoid it in the first place. Contact your creditors at the first sign of trouble and request to have your payments temporarily reduced or postponed. Most companies will be agreeable to this arrangement. The important point, however, is not to bury your head in the sand and pretend that the problem doesn't exist. Don't ignore your bills, especially when they become overdue.

If you are already beyond this point, the following are five choices to consider.

DEBT CONSOLIDATION

This is a method of paying off all your bills by borrowing a lump sum from a finance company. This is a popular approach to the problem of excessive debts, especially with the availability of low-interest home equity loans (since creditors will still loan money against your house despite a bad credit record). This plan may be worth considering if you are certain of receiving increased income during the next several years.

The advantages of this method are that it frees you from creditor harassment and gives you one monthly payment instead of many small bills. The disadvantages are that you will still be in debt and will now have additional interest charges to pay.

CONSUMER CREDIT COUNSELOR

Not to be confused with credit repair consultants, these are non-profit agencies that will help you analyze your financial difficulties and show you how to manage your personal finances. Their counselors will assist you in drawing up a budget and arranging more lenient repayment schedules. The fee for such assistance is nominal. Check the telephone directory for Consumer Credit Counseling Services, or contact the National Foundation for Consumer Credit, 8701 George Avenue, Suite 601, Silver Spring, Maryland, 20910.

WAGE EARNER'S PLAN, CHAPTER 13

This is a section of the Federal Bankruptcy Act designed for debt relief of anyone earning a living from wages, salaries, or commissions. Under the Wage Earner's Plan, you turn all your debts over to a federal court. The court then takes a portion of your income to pay your creditors.

This is a way to consolidate your debts, be protected by law, reduce your costs, and pay off your debts over a period of time. The court protects you from wage garnishment and other seizures during the repayment period. There is also a three-month grace period between the date of filing and your court date, during which time no payments are required of you. This plan can be filed with or without an attorney. There is a small filing fee and court fee required, and the forms can be purchased at a stationery store.

Despite these apparent advantages, the major drawback to filing a Chapter 13 is that it appears on your credit report as a form of bankruptcy. Most creditors consider this to be a major negative statement, and I recommend avoiding this method if at all possible.

BANKRUPTCY, CHAPTER 7

This should be your last resort—to be used only if you see no possible way of paying your debts and your credit is already so bad that one more major negative remark won't hurt it. Under Chapter 7, most of your debts will be discharged by the court and you will never have to repay them. Certain debts, however, are not dischargeable, such as taxes, alimony, child support, debts resulting from intentional injury to persons, damages to property, and debts obtained through fraud.

The major disadvantages of this method are:

• A bankruptcy statement will stay on your credit report for up to ten years.

• Because it is a public record item, it is one of the most difficult to have removed.

• You cannot file bankruptcy again for six years.

• Upon filing the petition, property belonging to the debtor (with the exception of certain property exempted by law) becomes part of the debtor's estate to be liquidated for distribution to creditors.

NEGOTIATION STRATEGY

This is my favorite. It is a win-win strategy in which the creditor agrees to accept a settlement as payment-in-full on your account. It also provides you with a way to maintain good credit. This method is further detailed in the next chapter.

Whichever method you use, I highly recommend that you begin today. Cut your expenses, increase your income, and do whatever it takes to free yourself of the burden of excessive debt. Get a clear picture of your financial situation and ability to repay your debts by completing the following monthly income statement and personal financial statement.

Monthly Income Statement

Net Income
    Salary (including spouse)
    Commissions & Bonuses
    Dividends
     Total:

Other Income
    Alimony; Child Support
    Real Estate & Investments
    Other
     Total:
     TOTAL INCOME:

Fixed Expenses
    Mortgage; Rent
    Property taxes
    Life & health insurance
    Property insurance
    Auto insurance
    Other insurance
    Utilities
     Total:

Variable Expenses
    Unsecured Loans
    Secured Loans
    Other loans
    Credit Cards; M/C, Visa, etc.
    Store credit cards
    T&E credit cards
    Taxes
    Other
     Total:

Medical; Dental
Transportation; Fuel; Repairs
Entertainment; Vacation
Food
Clothing
Savings
Charity
Other
  Total:
  TOTAL MONTHLY EXPENSES:

MONTHLY CASH FLOW
(INCOME MINUS EXPENSES):

Personal Financial Statement

Current Assets
  Cash on Hand
  Checking Account
  Savings Account
  Other Accounts
  Investments; Stocks; Bonds (liquid)
  Accounts Receivable
  Insurance (cash value)

Fixed Assets
  Real Estate
  Personal Property
  Automobiles
  Household Goods
  Retirement Plan
  Other
  TOTAL ASSETS:

<u>Short-Term Liabilities</u>
    Outstanding Bills
    Outstanding Credit Card Balances
    Taxes Owed
    Other

<u>Long-Term Liabilities</u>
    Mortgages
    Automobile Loans
    Installment Loans
    Margin on Stocks
    Other
      TOTAL LIABILITIES:

NET WORTH
(TOTAL ASSETS MINUS TOTAL LIABILITIES):

CHAPTER THREE

HOW TO ERASE BAD CREDIT

▼

This chapter offers a concise guide to erasing negative information from your credit reports. It is based on proven techniques used by attorneys and professional credit consultants to erase bad credit. The following is a summary of the most effective methods.

AUTOMATIC REMOVAL METHOD

The Fair Credit Reporting Act demands that derogatory items be removed after a specified period of time. By simply waiting long enough, most negative items on your credit report will be automatically removed. Unfortunately, seven years is the typical statute of limitations for reporting negative items. Bankruptcy may remain for as long as ten years. Positive information, on the other hand, remains for only five years. Doesn't quite seem fair, does it? Read on.

DISPUTE METHOD

This is the most common method used by professional credit consultants to remove negative information from your credit reports. For a $100 to $1,500 fee, the credit repair specialist will inform the various credit bureaus that certain items on your report are either incorrect, misleading, inaccurate, or obsolete. According to the Fair Credit Reporting Act, such items must be reinvestigated within a "reasonable amount of time" unless the dispute can be proven to be "frivolous and irrelevant." If, after reinvestigating, the credit bureau finds the disputed items to be incorrect, misleading, inaccurate, or obsolete, they must either correct or delete the information. This method can be very successful in removing derogatory items that were paid off years ago but still show a negative rating on your credit report.

The first step in utilizing the dispute method is to obtain a copy of your credit reports from the major bureaus in your area. Ask the bank or department store where you want to obtain credit for the names of the credit bureaus they report to. Or look in the Yellow Pages under Credit Bureaus or Credit Reporting Agencies. You can also seek assistance from a trade association called:

Associated Credit Bureaus
16211 Park Place 10
P.O. Box 218200
Houston, TX 77218
(713) 492-8155

Here is a list of the four largest credit bureaus in the United States:

TRW Credit Information Services
505 City Parkway West
Orange, CA 92667

Trans Union Credit Information
444 North Michigan Avenue
Chicago, IL 60611

CBI/Equifax
P.O. Box 4091
Atlanta, GA 30302

Associated Credit Services, Inc.
624 E. North Belt, Suite 400
Houston, TX 77060

The cost for a copy of your credit report usually ranges from $5 to $10. If you have been denied credit within the last thirty days because of negative information reported by one of the bureaus, you may obtain a free copy of your report from that bureau. Be sure to include your full name, address, Social Security number, and date of birth.

Once you have obtained a copy of your report, use the dispute form (the credit bureau will send you one along with your report) to indicate any items you believe to be incorrect, misleading, inaccurate, or obsolete, and return it to the credit bureau. If you do not receive a reply within six weeks, send a follow-up letter demanding immediate action. If the bureau does not remove all of the disputed items from your report, repeat the process.

The secret to success when disputing information is knowing how to word the dispute effectively. Do not make excuses for your actions, such as, "I was late because . . ." In some cases, an improperly worded dispute letter can cause the bureau to *add* negative information to your report.

Many credit repair clinics and mail-order credit courses use a form letter that they send to the various bureaus, disputing every negative item on the report. These form letters have recently been met with a form letter from the credit bureau stating "your dispute is frivolous and irrelevant."

The following are examples of successful disputes. Do not use them if they do not apply to your specific situation. My purpose in including them is to give you an idea of how to properly word your dispute.

Note: I do not advocate lying to a credit bureau regarding legitimate items on your report. You do, however, have a right to dispute any item that you reasonably believe to be inaccurate. Such inaccuracies may include wrong account numbers or dates, incorrect balances, or late payments. Even bankruptcies and other public-record items that contain certain discrepancies can be legitimately disputed.

Examples

• I never filed bankruptcy for $(amount) on (date). Please delete this information.

• This account has always been paid as agreed. Please verify with the creditor and correct or delete the information.

• I never had an account with (name of company). This is not my account.

• My account (give number) with (name of creditor) is current with no late payments. Please correct.

• Please remove this checkpoint. My Social Security number is xxx-xx-xxxx. The number must have been mistakenly transposed by a clerk at the bank. My Social Security number is not xxx-yy-xxxx.

• This is not my judgment. Please remove this item from my report.

• I do not have two accounts with this creditor. Please investigate and correct.

• I never authorized this company to inquire into my credit history. Please remove this inquiry.

CONSUMER STATEMENT

If the reinvestigation does not resolve the dispute, the law permits you to submit a brief statement describing the details of the questionable information in your file. The credit bureau will usually limit the length of your statement to a maximum of 100 words. Once again, it is important to word your statement in such a manner as to indicate that you were not at fault or that there was a mistake made in the reporting of the information. The following is one example of a consumer statement:

"I do not believe that my payment record with the ABC Company is listed correctly. I usually pay my bills as soon as I receive them, but never later than two weeks after receipt. The information in my credit file stating that my account with the ABC Company was overdue and had been sent to a collection agency is incorrect. I believe the problem is the result of a clerical error and should have been corrected long ago."

CIRCUMVENTION STRATEGY

This method is a variation of the dispute method. It relies upon the "reasonable time" in which a credit bureau must investigate a disputed item. Simply put, this strategy involves sending your dispute letter to a branch office of the credit bureau in a different part of the country. In order to do this effectively, it is necessary to utilize an address in a different reporting zone. The purpose is to make it more difficult for the credit bureau to reinvestigate the item being disputed. Once again, if the disputed item cannot be verified within a reasonable time period, it must be deleted.

In my opinion, the ethics of this method are somewhat questionable. Nonetheless, it is one of the most effective methods of removing public-record items such as bankruptcies, tax liens, and judgments from your credit reports. Several variations of this method are detailed in Chapter Six.

Note: Do not use a post office box or mail forwarding service when utilizing this method. TRW keeps a record of all such mail services and may indicate a checkpoint on your credit report.

ALTERNATIVE DISPUTE

This method involves disputing the item directly with the creditor. By writing a letter to the company that reported the negative information, it is often possible to have the status of your account changed to a positive rating. This is especially effective with accounts that are several years old, as the information is more difficult to verify. It is also very effective in cases where there was defective merchandise or improper billing. Be sure to direct your letter to the manager or vice president in charge of consumer relations.

NEGOTIATION STRATEGY

This is the most ethical and most effective of all methods that I know of. It is used to correct items that have not yet been paid off, and it is a win-win strategy.

The negotiation strategy involves calling your creditor and agreeing to pay the debt (or a percentage of the debt) in exchange for his agreement to change your credit rating to a positive remark. Changing the reported item to "paid collection account" or "paid charge-off" are *not* positive ratings, by the way. "Paid satisfactorily" or "current account" are examples of positive ratings.

Successful negotiation begins with an agreement by the creditor to accept as full settlement a specified amount of money (70 percent is a good target figure) in exchange for removing the derogatory item. Again, it is important to communicate with someone in charge. It is also important to make sure that your negotiation letter is properly worded and signed by all principals *before* you pay. The following is a sample settlement agreement that can be modified for your particular situation:

Address
Date

Attention:
Name of Creditor
Address

RE: Account #_____

Dear:

The purpose of this letter is to confirm our previous telephone conversation on (date) regarding the settlement of the above account.

In accordance with our agreement on the telephone, I will pay your company the amount of $_____ as full settlement of this account.

Upon the receipt of the above consideration, your company has agreed to change the remark on my credit file to "paid satisfactory." In addition, any references to late payment or charge-off regarding this account will be deleted from my file.

Your cooperation in this matter is greatly appreciated, and if this settlement agreement is acceptable to your company, please so acknowledge with your signature in the space provided below and return a copy to me. Upon receipt of this signed acknowledgment, I will immediately forward you a cashier's check in the amount stated above. Thank you very much for your immediate attention to this matter.

_____

(Signature of Authorized Officer)   (Date)

Yours sincerely,

Your name

LEGAL ACTION

It is important to know your rights under the various federal and state laws regarding credit. These laws include the Fair Credit Reporting Act, Equal Credit Opportunity Act, Truth in Lending Act, Fair Credit Billing Act, and Fair Debt Collector Practices Act. By understanding your rights under these laws, you can prevent creditors and credit bureaus from taking advantage of you.

If, for example, a credit bureau refuses to reinvestigate a disputed item, you may be able to file a complaint with the Federal Trade Commission as well as with the Attorney General. You may also be entitled to collect damages for violation of your rights under the Fair Credit Reporting Act.

Improper billing and unfair debt collection practices can also give you a right to file suit. In such cases, it may be wise to consult a competent attorney or consumer advocate. An attorney can file a motion for injunctive relief. This motion can lead to a court order for the credit bureau to temporarily refrain from listing all negative items being disputed until the case is resolved (which may be several years). It is also possible to file a complaint in small claims court without an attorney. Be sure to maintain complete records of all correspondence to back your claim.

The following are summaries of your rights under the various credit laws.

Fair Credit Reporting Act

1. To be told the nature and sources of the information collected about you by a credit bureau.

2. To obtain this information free of charge when you have been denied credit, insurance, or employment within the preceding 30 days. Otherwise, the reporting agency can charge a reasonable fee for the disclosure.

3. To be accompanied by anyone of your choosing when visiting the credit bureau.

4. To be told who has received your credit report within the preceding six months, or within the preceding two years if the report was furnished for employment purposes.

5. To have incomplete, incorrect, or obsolete information reinvestigated and, if found to be inaccurate or unverifiable, to have the information removed from your file.

6. When a dispute between you and the credit bureau cannot be resolved, to have your version of the dispute placed in the file and included in future reports.

7. To request that the credit bureau send your consumer statement to all future credit grantors.

8. To have a credit report withheld from anyone who does not have a legitimate business need for the information contained in it.

9. To sue a company for damages if it willfully or negligently violates the law, and if the suit is successful, to collect attorneys' fees and court costs.

10. To be notified if a company is requesting an investigative consumer report.

11. To request from an investigating company further information as to the nature and scope of the investigation.

12. To have negative information removed from your report after seven years. One major exception is bankruptcy, which may be reported for ten years.

Equal Credit Opportunity Act

1. To find out the reasons for credit denial.

2. To receive credit in your own name.

3. To refuse to answer questions about childbearing plans or birth control practices.

4. To have equal consideration of all credit criteria,

including income between the sexes, in determining creditworthiness.

5. To have alimony, child support, and separate maintenance considered as any other income.

Truth In Lending Act

1. To be given a complete, written explanation of both the annual percentage rate (APR) being charged for any credit transactions and the total dollar amount of the transaction, except for mortgages.

Fair Credit Billing Act

1. To withhold payment of any disputed portion of a billing until the creditor resolves the dispute.

2. To receive acknowledgment from a creditor within 30 days.

3. To have the creditor resolve a dispute within two billing cycles.

Fair Debt Collection Practices Act

1. To receive verification from the debt collector of the amount that you owe.

2. To not be harassed or threatened by a debt collector.

The Federal Trade Commission is the agency responsible for enforcing all of the above regulations. If a company has violated your rights under any of these laws, you can file a complaint with the nearest regional office. Address your inquiries to "Director," FTC headquarters, at:

Federal Trade Commission
Pennsylvania Avenue & Sixth Street, N.W.
Washington, D.C. 20580
(202) 523-3830

The following are addresses for FTC regional offices:

1718 Peachtree St. N.W., Suite 1000, Atlanta, GA 30367
150 Causeway St., Room 1301, Boston, MA 02114
118 St. Clair Ave., Suite 500, Cleveland, OH 44114
20001 Bryan St., Suite 2665, Dallas, TX 75201
11000 Wilshire Blvd., Los Angeles, CA 90024
1405 Curtis St., Suite 2900, Denver, CO 80202
26 Federal Plaza, Room 2243-EB, New York, NY 10278
450 Golden Gate Ave., San Francisco, CA 94102
912 2nd Ave., 28th Floor, Seattle, WA 98174

FILE SEGREGATION

I consider this to be the most abused and perhaps most controversial of all methods used to erase bad credit. At the same time, it is the most powerful, dynamic, and effective method for *totally* erasing negative credit information virtually overnight.

Because of the sensitive nature of this particular technique, I recommend contacting a reputable credit consultant or attorney. They may be able to assist you in establishing a brand new credit file for a fee between $1,000 and $3,000. The following agencies can refer you to a reputable professional in your area:

Consumer Advocate Law Center
210 N. Central, #215
Glendale, CA 91203
(818) 500-7878

Consumer Credit Commission
4286 Redwood Highway, #350
San Rafael, CA 94903
(415) 491-4152

A complete description of the file segregation method, including the identification systems used by all of the major credit bureaus in the United States, is contained in Chapter Six.

WHICH METHODS TO USE

Different approaches are called for depending on the particular problem involved. The list below outlines typical credit problems and the best methods (listed in order of effectiveness) to eliminate the problem.

Late payment (6, 5, 2)
Collection account (6, 5, 2)
Charge-off (6, 2)
Paid collection (2, 5)
Paid charge-off (2, 5)
Repossession (6, 2)
Bankruptcy (4, 2)
Defaulted student loan; unpaid (6, 2)
Defaulted student loan; paid (2)
Tax lien (6, 4, 2, 3)
Judgment (6, 7, 4, 2, 3)
CHECKPOINT/TRANS ALERT/CAUTION (2, 7)
Inquiry (5, 2, 7)

1. Automatic Removal
2. Dispute Method
3. Consumer Statement
4. Circumvention Strategy
5. Alternative Dispute
6. Negotiation Strategy
7. Legal Action
8. File Segregation

Note: File segregation is the only 100 percent effective method to erase all negative items from your credit report. It is not, however, recommended or necessary for most cases.

CHAPTER FOUR
YOUR CREDIT APPLICATION
AND OBTAINING AAA-1 CREDIT

▼

This book would not be complete without a discussion of credit applications and the secrets of obtaining new credit. In addition to reviewing your credit reports, the prospective lender will evaluate the information supplied on your application. Basically, there are four elements that the prospective lender will consider before extending you credit. They are:

    1. *Collateral.* What type of security do you have to offer?

    2. *Character.* This includes work history, residential information, and so on.

    3. *Credit.* Other accounts and/or references.

    4. *Capacity.* Ratio of debt to income, available cash flow, savings, and so on.

Most creditors use a point system to evaluate your application in relation to the above "4-Cs." Elements of your application are assigned a certain number of points depending upon how you answer each question. In some cases, a high-scoring application can offset a negative credit history reflected in your credit report. In other instances, a low-scoring credit application may negate an otherwise excellent credit history.

For example, a person with a previous bankruptcy may still be able to obtain credit if he can demonstrate sufficient income, stable job history, established residence, and other good credit references. On the other hand, a person with an excellent credit report may be denied credit if the application shows that he or she is new to the area with a new job and a high debt-to-income ratio.

POINT SCORING SYSTEM

The following is an example of a point system used by a number of credit grantors, including major banks and department stores.

CATEGORY	POINTS
AGE GROUP:	
18 - 25	1
26 - 64	2
65 and over	1
DEPENDENTS:	
None	0
1 - 3	2
4 or more	1
TELEPHONE LISTED IN APPLICANT'S NAME	2

STABILITY:
0 - 5 years at present address	1
5 years or more at present address	2

PREVIOUS ADDRESS:
5 years or less	1
More than 5 years	2

EMPLOYMENT:
1 year or less at present employment	1
1 - 3 years at present employment	2
4 - 6 years at present employment	3
7 - 10 years at present employment	4
11 years or more at present employment	5
Spouse employed if applying jointly	2

CREDIT EXPERIENCE:
Loan with this bank	5
Loan with another bank	3
Checking or savings account with this bank	3
Checking or savings account at another bank	2

TYPE OF WORK:
Professional or Executive	4
Skilled Worker	3
Blue Collar	2
All others	1

MONTHLY OBLIGATIONS (INCLUDING RENT/MORTGAGE):
Less than $750	2
More than $750	1

18 Points or more: Pass

15 - 17 Points: Borderline (subject to review)
15 or less: Fail (automatic rejection)

THE PRINCIPAL REASONS FOR CREDIT DENIAL

1. Credit application incomplete
2. Insufficient credit references
3. Unable to verify credit references
4. No credit file
5. Insufficient credit file
6. Delinquent credit obligations
7. Length of employment
8. Unable to verify employment
9. Temporary or irregular employment
10. Insufficient income
11. Unable to verify income
12. Excessive obligations
13. Inadequate collateral
14. Too short a period of residence
15. Temporary residence
16. Unable to verify residence
17. Garnishments, attachment, foreclosure, repossession, or suit
18. Bankruptcy
19. We do not grant credit to any applicant on the terms you request
20. Other (specified)

The following occupations are considered to be less than stable by the majority of credit grantors:

Actor
Attendant
Barber
Bartender
Beautician

Cook
Domestic
Hospital orderly
House painter
Laborer
Musician
Nurse's aide
Porter
Practical nurse
Self-employed (most creditors equate this with being
  unemployed)
Taxi driver
Waitress
Window cleaner

OBTAINING A VISA OR MASTERCARD

One of the most important tools in your journey toward
AAA-1 credit is a Visa or MasterCard. A major credit card
is often necessary in order to cash a check or rent a car. It
also serves as an excellent reference when applying for
credit elsewhere. Unfortunately, the requirements for such
credit cards are usually quite strict at most banks and
savings institutions.

Now there is a way to obtain a Visa or MasterCard
regardless of your previous credit history. A secured credit
card is offered by some companies when you deposit a
specified amount of money as security. The required bal-
ance varies with each institution. The following is a list of
financial institutions that offer secured credit cards:

Service One International
21032 Devonshire, Suite 215
Chatsworth, CA 91311
1-800-331-1900

New Era Bank
P.O. Box 15414
Wilmington, DE 19850-5414
(201) 937-5000

Berthoud National Bank
P.O. Box 3057
Omaha, NE 68103-3057
(215) 524-8740

Key Federal
153 Chestnut Hill Road
Newark, DE 19713
(302) 454-1919

Heritage Exchange
301 Plymouth Drive N.E.
Dalton, GA 30720
(404) 259-6035

Citicorp Savings of Illinois
P.O. Box 87581
Chicago, IL 60680
(312) 997-5720

Pioneer First Federal Savings & Loan
4111 200th Street, S.W.
Lynwood, WA 98036
(206) 771-2525

Standard Savings & Loan
888 North Hill Street
Los Angeles, CA 90012
(213) 617-8688

Great American First Savings Bank
P.O. Box 85096
San Diego, CA 92138
(619) 231-1885

First Consumers National Bank
Lincoln Center Tower
P.O. Box 2088
Portland, OR 97208-2088
1-800-876-3262

HOW TO ESTABLISH AAA-1 CREDIT

The following system is a step-by-step method to build your credit, regardless of your past history.

1. Obtain copies of your credit report from each of the major bureaus in your area.

2. Use the methods outlined in Chapter Three to erase the negative items from your report.

3. Reduce your outstanding debts as much as possible using the negotiation strategy.

4. Open a savings and checking account at a well-known bank (not a savings and loan or credit union).

5. Obtain a secured credit card from one of the companies listed on pages 33-35.

6. Using your secured credit card as a reference, open an account with a major furniture or department store.

7. Establish a $1,000 certificate of deposit account at the bank where you opened your account.

8. After two to three months, ask the bank to loan you $1,000 using your CD account as collateral.

9. Accelerate payment on all of your accounts by making your payments ahead of schedule.

10. Apply for a major unsecured credit card.

CHAPTER FIVE

HOW TO MAKE $100,000 A YEAR AS A PROFESSIONAL CREDIT CONSULTANT

▼

As I mentioned earlier, 70 percent of adult consumers in this country have some type of negative item on their credit reports. Most of these individuals don't have the time or the know-how to effectively repair their own credit without the help of a professional. Just as with problems with cars, plumbing, health, or legal affairs, most people would rather pay a professional than deal with these situations alone.

That's where the services of a professional credit consultant come in. Credit consultants have been known to charge $50 to $150 for a simple analysis of a credit report with specific recommendations. The fee for actually cleaning up a credit report ranges between $100 to $1,500 per report, depending upon the number and type of derogatory items. For using the file segregation method to help a person "start over" with a new credit file, fees between $1,000 and $3,000 are not uncommon.

Based on these kinds of fees, can you see how easy it would be for an aggressive consultant to earn up to $100,000 a year or more? In addition, most credit consultants combine their credit repair business with other related financial services, such as loan brokerage, real estate investment, or financial planning. Due to the recent negative publicity about credit repair clinics, many consultants are now keeping their credit repair business low profile and secondary to their other services. These individuals rely mostly upon word-of-mouth to generate new business.

On the other hand, many credit consultants advertise in the classified sections of the newspaper and in the Yellow Pages. They also conduct seminars and promote their services on television. By operating ethically and aboveboard, they maintain completely legitimate organizations. The services of an honest credit repair specialist are in high demand and therefore command the same fees received by successful attorneys, physicians, and other professionals.

At the time of this writing, there are no special educational or licensing requirements for credit consultants. All that is needed is a good understanding of the methods outlined in this book and a business license. This is subject to change in the future as a few "bad apples" give the rest of the consultants a bad name. For this reason it is advisable to obtain a surety bond as well as membership in such organizations as the Better Business Bureau, Chamber of Commerce, or Consumer Credit Commission.

You will also need contracts, letterhead stationery, and business cards. At the same time, it is imperative to continue your education in the various aspects of credit repair by attending seminars, buying special reports, and subscribing to specialized newsletters. All of this will keep you up-to-date on the latest developments in the industry and add greatly to your credibility.

Regarding office space, it is best to start out with a shared office suite until you can afford your own private office. A good arrangement would be to share space with other financial professionals, such as mortgage brokers, accountants, or attorneys. You may even be able to work out some kind of referral network with the other members of your suite.

Another way to conduct business that eliminates the high overhead of the previous arrangement is to operate out of your own home. In fact, it is possible to conduct your business entirely by mail, without even meeting your clients. This way of doing business opens up unlimited opportunities, and I highly recommend considering it.

What you are really doing is selling information. By developing a relationship with a local independent bureau, you can obtain instant credit reports for your clients via FAX machine. They will probably charge you about $10 to $15 per report. You can then sell the report, along with a complete written analysis and specific recommendations, for $100 or more. You can provide follow-up consultations and assistance for an additional fee. Again, this type of enterprise can be run entirely by mail from the privacy of your own home. As you expand, you can market related materials to your clients, such as secured credit cards, specialized reports, or even your own monthly newsletter.

CHAPTER SIX
FILE SEGREGATION

▼

A couple in Riverside, California, was recently turned down for a mortgage on a new home as a result of a previous bankruptcy. They came to me for a consultation, desperate for a way to reestablish their credit within a short period of time. After doing a complete analysis of their credit reports and present financial situation, I suggested that they consider creating a new credit file. I then referred them to one of my close associates, who assisted them in establishing a completely new credit line within a matter of days. A month later they invited me to a housewarming at their new $480,000 home.

The purpose of this chapter is to reveal the intricacies of the file segregation method of credit repair. While perhaps the most unorthodox, it is certainly a powerful, dynamic, and effective method to totally erase a person's negative credit history. It is also the only completely legal method of erasing bad credit overnight.

This amazing technique is so effective that some consultants charge fees of up to $3,000 to set up new files for their clients. It is particularly attractive to people whose credit is so bad that it would take at least a year to repair using the conventional methods. It is sometimes used as a temporary measure in order to obtain immediate credit or financing while the old file is being cleaned up. By utilizing the file segregation method, it is possible to create a brand new credit file (with no connection to the previous record) in as little as five minutes.

File segregation allows a person to literally "start over" with a credit report that states NO RECORD FOUND. Credit information can then be added to a new file, thereby allowing a person to establish an excellent credit record within a short period of time.

The secret of file segregation is circumventing, or bypassing, the identification system used by major credit bureaus. Unfortunately, each bureau has its own particular series of file identifiers. Therefore, it is necessary to circumvent all of the bureaus' identification systems simultaneously in order to produce the desired result.

Many people have tried to bypass the system by altering the spelling of their name, changing their Social Security number, or lying about their date of birth. These methods are generally ineffective and will often result in the addition of a CHECKPOINT, TRANS ALERT, or CAUTION to a report. These are all indicators used by major credit bureaus to identify potential fraud. In some cases a person may end up with several CHECKPOINTS on his credit report, resulting in even worse credit than before.

In other cases, individuals have tried "borrowing" the credit of someone else with a similar name. A recent article in *Newsweek* (September 12, 1988) reported that certain unethical credit repair clinics were selling the credit histories of people with good credit to people with bad credit. This is illegal and resulted in the arrests of dozens of credit thieves and greedy consumers.

The only legitimate way to start over is to create a brand new credit file using the methods outlined in this chapter. First, it will be necessary to describe the identification systems used by each of the major bureaus. Then you will learn how to circumvent these systems using a variety of strategies.

Once you have learned to create a new file, you'll need to establish a positive credit history. The subsection entitled *How To Establish AAA-1 Credit In 30 Days* (page 54) reveals a virtually unknown technique that has been used by undercover FBI agents to add several accounts with five to ten years of excellent credit history to newly created files. Not a rehash of old methods, this is a totally new approach to establishing an "instant" line of credit.

HOW FILE SEGREGATION WAS DISCOVERED

Several years ago, two Los Angeles attorneys discovered a weak link in the file retrieval system used by the major credit bureaus. They noticed that in certain cases, no record was found for a particular individual, and subsequently a new file was automatically created by the credit bureau. In some cases, one person would have several files existing simultaneously, each with different information.

When the attorneys noticed that there were many more credit files than there were consumers, they realized that the weak link was in the file identification system itself. Legal research determined that the creation of additional files did not in itself constitute an illegal act—the only exception would be if the additional credit file was used to commit fraud.

The attorneys decided to capitalize on this idea when they were presented with a credit file that appeared to be beyond the scope of conventional credit repair methods.

Instead of going through the dispute process and waiting for the negative information to be deleted, and rather than negotiating settlement agreements with creditors, they simply created a brand new credit file.

They began charging fees between $3,000 and $4,000 to create new files for their clients, or rather, to advise their clients on the creation of new files. This information has been passed on to a select number of credit consultants who typically charge $1,000 to $3,000 or more to help their clients "start over."

IDENTIFICATION SYSTEMS
OF THE MAJOR BUREAUS

Every credit bureau has a particular system of file retrieval that allows them to identify the file of each person in that system. It is necessary to identify each file in such a manner as to separate individuals with similar names and addresses, so that Robert Hammond will not appear on the file of Bob Hammond. However, no bureau has yet come up with a perfect system of file identification. That is why you will sometimes see items on your report that belong to someone else with a similar name.

In an effort to maintain maximum efficiency, credit bureaus prefer to set up more than one file per person rather than risk merging several people's files into one. This is the "weak link" that allows a person to circumvent the system.

In my research, I have discovered two basic types of file identification systems. The first system (Type A) is used by TRW, CBI/Equifax, and other major credit bureaus with the exception of Trans Union. The second system (Type B) is used mainly by Trans Union.

Type A File Identification System
The following sequence of information is entered into

the computer in an attempt to match an existing file. If the information does not match, a new file is created.

1. *Last name*. The computer only recognizes the first ten digits of the last name. Letters must match an existing file, or a new file will be created and the computer will stop the search. Otherwise the computer will proceed.

2. *First name*. If the last name matches an existing file, the computer will continue by matching the first three letters of the first name. If the first name matches an existing file with the same first name and last name, it will then proceed to match other elements. Otherwise a new file will be created.

3. *Middle initial*. Once the last name and first name have been matched, the computer will proceed to match the middle initial. If all elements match, the program will continue. Otherwise it will either create a new file or skip the middle initial and proceed with the checking.

4. *Spouse*. If married, the spouse's first initial will appear after the file holder's middle initial. If not married, the computer will proceed to match other elements.

5. *House number*. After matching all the above elements, the computer will proceed to match the first five digits of the house number and continue.

6. *Street name*. The computer will proceed by matching the first letters of the street name.

7. *Zip code*. The computer will proceed to match address with zip code. If five years or more at present address, the computer will stop. A search revealing persons with similar names and addresses will result in the files being merged and a CHECKPOINT entry added to the file.

8. *Previous address*. If less than five years at present address, the computer will check previous addresses. The computer can hold up to ten previous addresses, but will usually list only the last three.

9. *Social Security number.* The computer will proceed to match all of the previous elements with the Social Security number. If the Social Security number does not match the previously reported number, a CHECKPOINT will be entered.

Type B File Identification System

This system is based entirely on the applicant's Social Security number. If it does not match the name, a new file will be created.

Due to the fact that there are several different identification systems used by major credit bureaus, some creditors will run a report from two or three bureaus before granting credit or large purchases such as cars or real estate. In most cases, however, the creditor will rely on only one bureau. By learning the name of the bureau before applying for credit, it is possible to circumvent that bureau's identification system using the methods in this chapter. It is also possible to circumvent the identification systems of all the major credit bureaus simultaneously.

The following is a list of the four largest U.S. credit bureaus:

TRW Credit Information Services
P.O. Box 5450
Orange, CA 92613-5450
(714) 937-2000

Trans Union Credit Information
444 N. Michigan Avenue
Chicago, IL 60611
(312) 645-6000

CBI/Equifax
P.O. Box 4091
Atlanta, GA 30302
(404) 329-1725

Associated Credit Systems, Inc.
P.O. Box 52639
Houston, TX 77052
(800) 231-6703

CIRCUMVENTION STRATEGIES

The most comprehensive method of file segregation will circumvent all of the major credit bureaus in the United States simultaneously. This is accomplished by using a different first or last name, a different address, and a different Social Security number. It is important to avoid using any of your previous identifying information on future credit applications.

You may, however, only need to change one or two of these identifiers to bypass the identification system you will be facing. The following are methods to circumvent the Type A file identification system:

1. *Different last name.* This method has been used successfully by women whose last name has been changed through marriage or divorce. By resorting to the maiden name, it is often possible to circumvent the file that was created during marriage. It is important to never disclose the other last name on future credit applications, or the two files will merge. A woman with a negative credit history can marry a man with good credit, and by changing her name it is possible to create a new credit file overnight.

2. *Different first name and different address.* This is the most common method of file segregation used by credit consultants to bypass Type A file identification systems.

Since most people object to actually changing their first name, it is usually done by using the middle name as the first name and the first name as the middle initial. For example, if your name is John David Rockefeller, you can use David J. Rockefeller. This method will not work if the first letter of your middle name is the same as the first letter of your first name.

It is also essential to combine the change of first name with a change of address. Do not use your present address or any of your previous addresses on any credit applications or you will merge with your old file.

3. *Different first name, different last name.* This is accomplished by using one of the methods described in the subsection on alternate identities.

The following are methods to circumvent the Type B file identification system:

1. *Applying for a new Social Security number.* This is done according to the Department of Health, Education and Welfare's publication, *Records, Computers, and The Rights of Citizens.* The Social Security Act provides that "Any employee may have his account number changed at any time by applying to the Social Security Board and showing good reason for the change. With that exception, only one account number will be assigned to an employee."

One individual used this method successfully by informing the manager of the local Social Security office that someone else had illegally used his name and Social Security number to make unauthorized credit purchases. The manager accepted this as a "good reason" and authorized a new number.

On another occasion, a man requested a new Social Security number be issued because of his previous arrest record. He told them that he did not want his arrest records accessible to any other data files that use the Social Security number as a primary identifier. Again, the request for a new number was granted.

2. *Make up a new Social Security number.* This is a common technique used by individuals such as illegal aliens who do not have the legal right to work in the United States. It is important to note that each set of digits has a certain significance. The first three digits correspond to the state in which the card is applied for. The second two digits represent the approximate year of issue. The final four digits are used as personal identifiers.

3. *Typographical error on the credit application.* Often an individual will "accidently" transpose a couple of numbers in his Social Security number on his credit application. Example: 555-12-3456 to 555-12-4356.

4. *Apply for a Social Security number under an alternate identity.* This is a highly unorthodox method used by individuals who have obtained an alternate identity using one of the methods outlined later in this chapter. The legality of this method is somewhat questionable, and I would recommend consulting an attorney before proceeding.

CREATING A NEW FILE

Once a person has decided on a particular circumvention strategy, the only thing that has to be done is to establish the new file at each major credit bureau. This is accomplished by ordering a copy of your credit report using the new identifying information. Appendix B contains an example of a letter used to order a credit report.

It is also possible to order all of your credit reports directly from a small local bureau that can have the information FAX'd and available to you instantly. Of course, the fee for such instant credit reports is more than if you obtained them directly from the major bureaus yourself.

Another method is to apply for credit at a department store or auto dealer using the circumvention information in your application.

If your file segregation has been successful, your credit reports will come back marked NO RECORD FOUND. This means you have created a brand new credit file.

FOLLOW-UP PROCEDURE

Once you have successfully bypassed the identification systems of the major bureaus, it is important to follow up with these procedures:

1. Obtain a new driver's license. If you claim that you have lost your driver's license, you may apply for a new one for a modest fee. When applying for your new license, use your new name on the application—your license number will remain the same. In many states you don't need to show proof of your new name.

2. Open a savings and checking account under your new name and address. Use your new driver's license as identification.

3. Have the payroll department make your paychecks out to your new name. If your employer asks why, simply show them your new driver's license and tell them it is a personal family matter.

SPECIAL CIRCUMVENTION STRATEGIES

1. *Public record strategy.* Public records (such as bankruptcies, judgments, liens, and foreclosures) are listed by name and Social Security number. If the Social Security number does not match, the public records will not be identified. A typographical error in your Social Security number on the public record will prevent that record from being identified by any of the credit bureaus. If, for example, your lawyer's secretary accidentally transposed the

digits in your Social Security number on your petition for bankruptcy (e.g. 555-12-3456 to 555-21-3456), the bankruptcy will not appear on any of your credit reports.

2. *"Missing File" strategy.* Send a dispute letter to each of the major credit bureaus indicating that the bankruptcy on your report is inaccurate. Wait about a week, then go to the district court where your bankruptcy was filed and request to review your file. If the bankruptcy is several years old, the records will be stored in a federal archive center. Therefore, it may take a couple of weeks for the records to be shipped from the federal archives to the office of the court clerk.

When your records arrive, wait until the court clerk informs you that the records will be sent back to the federal archives unless you come down to review them. Ask for an extension. During this time, your bankruptcy records will be placed in a holding area. After you have reviewed your records, they will be packed up and shipped back to the federal archives.

This entire process will cause your records to be in transit for a period of four to six weeks.

According to the Fair Credit Reporting Act, the credit bureaus must verify any disputed items by contacting the source of the information. If the information cannot be verified, it must be deleted from your credit report. If the bureau does not respond within a "reasonable time," send them a follow-up letter indicating that if they cannot verify the information, it must be deleted immediately.

3. *Metamorphosis.* Another technique is to contact the credit bureaus where you have negative reports and inform them they have inaccurate information listed in the section where they identify the consumer. This could include such information as your name, address, and Social Security number. After the credit bureau changes its report

to reflect the new information, wait a few weeks before contacting the bureau again. Then write a dispute letter indicating that the negative remarks listed are not your accounts. Be sure to use the new identifying information.

The credit bureau must contact the creditors (as required by the Fair Credit Reporting Act) to verify the disputed information. When they discover that the information does not match, they will delete the negative information from your file. Several months later you can contact the bureau again and have them correct the identification information. By this time the report will reflect a clear credit history.

ALTERNATE IDENTITIES

1. *Use method.* This is a legal method of changing your name. No court appearance is required. All that is necessary is to begin using a new name of your choosing. Simply begin using your new name for all of your records and transactions. Be sure to obtain a new driver's license from the Department of Motor Vehicles.

This is the same method used by a woman who gets married and begins using her husband's name. The same is true when a divorced woman chooses to return to her maiden name.

See Appendix C for an example of a form that can assist you in utilizing this method. Simply fill it out, have it notarized, and present it to the offices where you would like to change your records. Appendix D contains an example of a similar form that can be used by a divorced woman who chooses to return to her former legal name. Once a person has established a new identity in one state, he may transfer this information to another state.

2. *Court method.* This is a more common way of creating a new identity. An attorney may file the required

forms and accompany you to court, or you may do all the paperwork yourself. The court will ask you questions about your reasons for changing your name. Their main concern is that you are not assuming an alternative identity for fraudulent purposes. In California the fee for a legal name change is $95. The fees in other states may vary. If there is no reason why the name change should not be approved, the court will grant the name change. A copy of the declaration will be forwarded to the Secretary of State.

Both of these methods are legal ways to change your name. As an adult citizen of the United States, you have the right to use any name you choose, providing that it is not used with the intent to defraud and that it does not interfere with the rights of another person (such as using the name of a famous entertainer or public figure).

Once again, it is important to change the name on your driver's license (a simple process involving filling out a form at the local Department of Motor Vehicles) and open a bank account under your new name.

Note: Changing your name does not affect your legal liability or past debts. You are still liable for all past and future debts incurred under your original name. A name change does not relieve you of your debts or responsibilities. For further information on alternate identities, I highly recommend *The Paper Trip*, available from Eden Press, and *New ID in America* from Paladin Press.

3. *Address change*. The Constitution of the United States also protects your right to live at any address or to use any address as your mailing address. In order to do this for the purposes of file segregation, you have three choices: move to a new address; use the address of a friend or relative; use a mail receiving service.

In order to use the file segregation method successfully, it is important to never reveal any of your previous addresses when completing future applications. This would result in your old file merging with your new file, thus defeating your purpose.

Note: TRW has recently begun compiling a list of mail receiving services. If you use one, it may show up on your credit report.

HOW TO ESTABLISH AAA-1 CREDIT IN 30 DAYS

This secret technique was developed by a former security chief of one of the major credit bureaus. It came about as a result of a need by undercover FBI agents to establish an instant credit history when working under an assumed name.

The secret to this method is to apply to banks where you already have credit under your old name and ask them to issue an additional secondary card to the new name and address, with the original signer of that account as guarantor. The bank will issue the card without hesitation, since the person guaranteeing the second card has a good payment history with that account.

The result is that the complete history of that credit card account, including the date the account was opened and the payment record, will appear on the new file without any notation that it is a secondary card. This results in the addition of up to ten years of excellent credit history on your brand new credit file in a matter of weeks.

A variation of this method is to have a trusted friend or family member with good credit request an additional card be issued in your new name. One way to convince them to do this is to let them know that they can have the card back cut in half as soon as you receive it.

You do not need to use the card itself in order for this technique to work. Be sure, however, that this person has had an excellent payment history with that particular account. Otherwise you will "inherit" a history of late payments. It may be wise to have your friend order a credit report first to make certain that the account has been reported accurately. By requesting additional cards from several sources, it is possible to establish AAA-1 credit in less than thirty days.

Appendix E illustrates a sample request letter. Once this letter has been sent, you will receive either a secondary credit card or a credit application for the secondary card. If you receive an application, have your friend fill out the applicant information and you complete the information under the co-applicant category. Send in the application and wait for your new card.

After you have received your secondary cards, wait a few weeks and order your credit reports from each of the major bureaus. Your reports should reflect the credit histories of that account. This process can be repeated with several major credit and department store cards, and the credit history established by the primary cardholder will appear in your new file.

This technique can also be used when your friend or family member applies for a new credit card. All you need to do is have them add your name as an additional card holder (not co-applicant) to the application.

SUMMING UP FILE SEGREGATION

In conclusion, I would like to emphasize that the methods outlined in this chapter are completely legal as long as there is no intent to defraud and as long as no one else's rights are violated. These techniques can help you start over by allowing you to obtain immediate financing while you work on clearing up your credit using the more conventional methods.

I would also like to remind you that creating a new

credit file does not relieve you of your previous debts or responsibilities. My hope is that once you have established credit under your new file, you will use your new financial standing wisely and take care of your obligations in an ethical manner.

How you use the information presented in this chapter is entirely up to you. I hope you will use it diligently and with caution. The services of a competent attorney are highly recommended before using any of these techniques.

CONCLUSION

▼

In conclusion, I would like to emphasize that the only long lasting way to clean up your credit is to *pay what you owe*. There is a universal principle that comes to your assistance when you are determined to become debt free. It is the law of compensation, which says, "There ain't no such thing as a free lunch!" Or better put, "Do unto others as you would have them do unto you."

Realize that the individuals and companies who gave you credit trusted you and believed in your ability to succeed. Your responsibility is to acknowledge that trust by believing in your own capabilities. Remember, the only limits are the ones you set for yourself!

Begin now by facing your responsibilities. Contact your creditors and negotiate a settlement agreement. You'll be amazed at how helpful they can become when they learn that you want to pay off your debts. If a company turns you down for credit, follow up with a letter asking them to reconsider your application based upon additional information. Let them know that in spite of a few mistakes, there are many reasons why you are now a good credit risk. If you don't have the time or patience to develop your own credit repair strategy as outlined in this book, contact a competent attorney or credit consultant to assist you.

Thank you for letting me share this information with you. My sincere desire is that you will not simply read it and forget about it. Rather, read it over several times and apply the information to your own situation. Feel free to write to me and share your testimonials. Good luck in all of your endeavors. May you live long and prosper!

OTHER RESOURCES

▼

BOOKS

An Investigative Research and Legal Opinion in the File Segregation Method
Consumer Advocate Law Center
210 N. Central, #215
Glendale, CA 91203

Credit: The Cutting Edge
by Scott French
CEP, Inc.
P.O. Box 865
Boulder, CO 80306

How To Use Mail Drops For Privacy and Profit
by Jack Luger
Loompanics Unlimited
P.O. Box 1197
Port Townsend, WA 98368

New ID In America
Paladin Press
P.O. Box 1307
Boulder, CO 80306

The Paper Trip (I and II)
by Barry Reid
Eden Press
P.O. Box 8410
Fountain Valley, CA 92728

ORGANIZATIONS

Consumer Advocate Law Center
210 N. Central, #215
Glendale, CA 91203

Consumer Credit Commission, Consumer
  Rights Organization
4286 Redwood Highway, #350
San Rafael, CA 94903

Hammond & Associates Financial Consultants
P.O. Box 1253
Moreno Valley, CA 92337

SAMPLE LETTER FOR ORDERING A CREDIT REPORT

▼

Date:

Credit Bureau
Address
City, State, Zip

Attention: Consumer Relations Department

To Whom It May Concern:

Please send me a copy of my current credit report. Enclosed is a money order in the amount of $8.00. *

Sincerely Yours,

Joe Chameleon
777 New Life Street
Start Over, CA 91111
SSN:123-45-6798
Date of Birth: 4-1-88

* $8.00 is the current price for credit reports in California.
Check with the bureau in your area for the cost of a credit
report.

DECLARATION OF LEGAL NAME CHANGE

▼

I, the undersigned, declare that the following is true and correct:

I, _____ (name currently using), born _____ (name on birth certificate), in _____ County in the state of _____ on the _____ day of _____ (month), _____ (year) DO HEREBY DECLARE my intent to change my legal name, and be henceforth exclusively known as _____ (new name).

NOTICE IS HEREBY GIVEN to all agencies of the State, all agencies of the Federal government, and creditors, and all private persons, groups, businesses, corporations, and associations of this legal change of name.

I declare that I am 18 years of age or older. I further declare that I have no intention of defrauding any person or escaping any obligation I may currently have by this act.

DATE: _____

X _____ (old signature)
X _____ (new signature)
State of _____
County of _____

On _____ (date), before me, _____
a notary public of the state of _____, known
to me to be a person whose name is subscribed to this
instrument, and acknowledged that he/she executed the
same.

_____
Notary Public for said State
(seal)
Date Notary Commission expires

DECLARATION RESTORING FORMER LEGAL NAME

▼

I, the undersigned, declare that the following is true and correct:

I, _____ (name presently using), was legally divorced in the state of _____ on _____ (date of divorce).

I HEREBY DECLARE my intent to return to my former legal name and be henceforth exclusively known as _____ (former name).

NOTICE IS HEREBY GIVEN to all agencies of this State, all agencies of the Federal government, all creditors and all private persons, groups, businesses, corporations, and associates of this legal change of name.

DATE: _____

X _____ (old signature)

X _____ (new signature)

State of _____

County of _____

On _____ (date), before me, _____, a notary public of the state of _____, personally appeared _____, known to me to be the person whose name is subscribed to this instrument, and acknowledged that he/she executed the same.

_____
Notary Public for said State
(seal)
Date Notary Commission expires

APPENDIX E
SAMPLE REQUEST LETTER

▼

Date

Name of Bank/Department Store
Credit Card Department
Address
City, State, Zip

Re: Name of previous cardholder
Address of primary cardholder
Account Number (of credit card)

To Whom It May Concern:

As the above named credit-card holder, I would like to request that a secondary card be issued to the following person. I will guarantee the payment on this account.

Name: Secondary card applicant
Address: Secondary applicant
Social Security number: Secondary applicant
Date of Birth: Secondary applicant

Your cooperation and immediate attention to this matter will be greatly appreciated.

Sincerely,

_____

Signature of primary cardholder